A code of practice for the detailed statement of accuracy

P J Campion
J E Burns
A Williams

NATIONAL PHYSICAL LABORATORY
Department of Trade and Industry

London   Her Majesty's Stationery Office   1973

SBN 11 480037 5

Preface

The precept that every measurement must be accompanied by an assessment of its uncertainty is introduced to experimental scientists early in their careers. That this teaching has borne fruit can be seen from a glance at the literature of the experimental physical sciences where the most frequent mathematical symbol to be seen is often the $\pm$ sign. However, when one attempts to use such statements of uncertainty it becomes evident that success in this matter is often more apparent than real. For example, it is unusual for any derivation of the uncertainty limits to be described, it is rare for sufficient information to be given for an assessment to be made of the significance of the difference between the reported result and some other measurement, and even more disappointing is the fact that the information given is likely to be ambiguous in its meaning.

The main purpose of this Code of Practice is to put forward recommendations as to how uncertainty can be expressed so as to avoid ambiguity. Further, it also discusses some of the ways in which estimates of uncertainty can be derived from individual measurements, including the separation into random and systematic categories, the procedures that can be adopted for combining the individual uncertainties in each category and the various ways in which acceptable statements of accuracy may be made. It is not a manual of statistics, nor does it deal with the subject of 'limits of error' as used in instrument specification. It is primarily concerned with the detailed reporting of scientific measurements of the highest quality, but the recommendations are such that they may be used for any situation where a statement of uncertainty is required, e.g. in certain calibration certificates, etc. However for those routine measurements in which the uncertainty of an instrument calibration is small, bearing in mind its subsequent use, it may be unnecessary to state the uncertainty in the detail required by this Code.

We are indebted to Longmans, Green and Co. for permission to adapt Table 1 from *Tables of Physical and Chemical Constants* (13th edition) by G. W. Kaye and T. H. Laby, and to the Literary Executor of the late Sir Ronald A. Fisher FRS, to Dr Frank Yates FRS, and to Oliver and Boyd, Edinburgh for permission to adapt Table 2 from their book *Statistical Tables for Biological, Agricultural and Medical Research*.

P J CAMPION
J E BURNS
A WILLIAMS

Contents

Section 1

Categories of uncertainties

The uncertainty of a measurement is often expressed quantitatively in the form $+x$, $-y$, or, more commonly, in the symmetrical form $\pm x$. It is clear, at least in a general way, what this pair of numbers means. It indicates the range of values about the final result within which the true value of the measured quantity is believed to lie. The clarification and amplification of this idea, and the ways in which x and y can be estimated and stated, are the main subjects of this booklet. Before taking them up, however, it is necessary to decide what the pair of numbers denoting uncertainty should be called. It is common practice to call it an error, as in the statement 'the estimated systematic error was $\pm 1\%$'. However, there is another terminology in widespread currency which uses instead an expression such as 'the estimated bounds of systematic error'. The difference is significant, since it reflects the view that, in accordance with its everyday meaning, the word *error* should be used to denote the amount by which a measured value departs from the true value; on this view, it is meaningless to say that an error is $\pm 1\%$.

This use of the word *error* to mean different things is a common source of confusion in scientific and technical writing, and is therefore discussed at some length in Appendix 1. However, it is unnecessary to go more deeply into the matter at this stage, since in this booklet the word *error* is used as little as possible, and only when there is no danger of ambiguity, as in the expression *standard error of the mean* which nowadays is a recognized and uniquely defined term in the language of statistics: the word *uncertainty* is used instead.

In this Code of Practice the uncertainty on a measurement is sub-divided as usual into two categories, i.e. the random uncertainty and the systematic uncertainty. As is described in Section 2 the random uncertainty is determined from a statistical analysis of repeated measurements that have been shown to be consistent with the Normal or other appropriate distribution.* Also, as is discussed in Section 3, the system-atic uncertainty is estimated from a consideration of the physical effects

---

* The verification that the observations are consistent with such a distribution is only possible for large numbers of observations and often a Normal distribution has to be assumed.

expected to influence or bias the result and, in those cases where repeated measurements do not follow a Normal or other appropriate law, from an assessment of the observed distribution. Furthermore, when the result of one experiment is being used in a subsequent experiment, the random uncertainty on the first result is included in the random uncertainty of the subsequent result, and similarly for the systematic uncertainties.

This can be contrasted with another approach that is also frequently used which, when the result of one experiment is being used in a subsequent experiment, includes the random uncertainty on the first result in the systematic uncertainty on the subsequent result. The basis for this is that any error (in the sense of deviation from true value) on the first result will cause a constant bias on the subsequent result. However, it is arguable that this is somewhat illogical, for the best estimate of this bias is zero with an uncertainty whose distribution is that of the random uncertainty on the first result.

An example may make this difference of approach clearer. Let us take the use of a physical constant in an experiment. On both procedures discussed above the random uncertainty on the measurement of the physical constant would be derived from the dispersion of the readings made in the determination of that constant. The two procedures diverge however when the value of this constant is needed in an experiment. On the second approach described above this *random* uncertainty on the value of the physical constant is taken as contributing to the *systematic* uncertainty on the result of the experiment, because any error in the value of the constant will cause a bias on the result of that experiment. Using the procedure adopted in this Code of Practice however, the *random* uncertainty on the estimate of the value of the physical constant is taken as contributing to the *random* uncertainty on the result of the experiment.

The latter procedure is more advantageous, since it leads to a more consistent way of treating uncertainties, in that a random uncertainty, derived from the dispersion of a set of readings, remains in the random category throughout all subsequent analyses and is not amalgamated with the much more subjectively assessed systematic uncertainties. In this way all the information available about random uncertainties is retained. Clearly, in order to reap the full benefit of this approach it is necessary to keep the two categories of uncertainties separate not only in the progressive combination of uncertainties throughout a complex experiment, but also in the statement of the final result.

Limits of estimation

The limit of estimation of an instrument is an example of an uncertainty that is usually systematic but which can, by change of experimental procedure, be replaced by a random uncertainty. Because of the importance of the underlying concept the example will be discussed in more detail.

Whatever kind of instrument is being used to make a measurement, the reading is always given to a limited number of significant figures. This particular limitation to the accuracy is known as the limit of estimation of the reading. For a digital instrument the limit of estimation is normally stated to be ± 1 in the last digit. For an analogue instrument the limit of estimation will depend as much on the observer's ability to estimate sub-divisions of scale intervals as on the scale itself.

Although the limit of estimation is usually assessed by such non-statistical means and is thus treated as a systematic uncertainty, this need not necessarily be the case. As an example consider the measurement of the length of an object using a rule with a scale graduated in equal divisions. Suppose that one end of the object is placed against the zero mark of the scale and that the other end is found to be nearest to the nth scale mark. Then the length lies between $n-\frac{1}{2}$ and $n+\frac{1}{2}$ scale divisions and however many times the measurement is repeated the result will always be the same. Under these circumstances the limit of estimation is a component of the systematic uncertainty. It has been assumed here that the limit of estimation is one scale division but in practice it is usually possible to read to a smaller interval by visually estimating subdivisions of the scale; the limit is now one subdivision of one scale interval but the above argument still holds.

It is however possible to randomize the limit of estimation by placing one end of the object, not at a fixed zero, but at points chosen at random near the lower end of the scale. Suppose the object has a true length $n+x$ scale intervals where x is less than one scale interval. When the object is placed at an arbitrary position on the scale it will be found to overlap either n or $n+1$ scale divisions, the probability of a reading n being $(1-x)$ and the probability of a reading $n+1$ being x. If R separate measurements are made and the object is placed at random on the scale each time, and, if r of the readings have a value n, then $R-r$ have a value $n+1$, and the ratio $(R-r)/R$ gives an unbiased estimate of x. In other words:

$$\text{length of object} = n + \frac{R-r}{R} \text{ scale divisions.}$$

Furthermore, the variance of the mean value from R measurements is given by $S^2(n+x) \approx \dfrac{r(R-r)}{R^3} \approx \dfrac{x(1-x)}{R}$

i.e. the standard error of the mean is inversely proportional to $\sqrt{R}$ for large R. (See JEFFREYS, H. *Scientific Inference*, 2nd edition, Cambridge University Press, 1957, 61.) Thus the precision attainable is limited only by the number of observations made, and hence the uncertainty becomes a component of the random uncertainty. If there are other additional causes of random variations in the readings then the value of the standard error of the mean will automatically include all such components. It should be noted that while the reduction in the random uncertainty is limited only by the number of measurements taken, in principle at least there will be residual systematic uncertainties due, for example, to the scale non-linearity of the ruler. For other analogue instruments the randomization can be achieved by resetting the zero of the instrument randomly at points near the lower end of the scale before each measurement is made. The concept is also applicable to digital instruments where, in some cases, the randomization is inherent in their operation.

Thus the above is an example of how, by a change of procedure, a subjectively assessed systematic uncertainty can be reduced at the expense of introducing a random uncertainty whose magnitude depends on the number of observations. In examining the accuracy that might be achieved in an experiment it is always worthwhile to consider whether the major components of the systematic uncertainty can be reduced by adopting randomization techniques similar to that described above.

Conclusions

In deciding whether an uncertainty is to be regarded as random or systematic, the criterion should be whether the values assigned to the uncertainty limits were derived from a statistical analysis of a number of measurements (assuming a Normal or other appropriate distribution), or whether it was possible only to estimate limiting values by a non-statistical assessment. It follows from this recommendation that, once they have been classified as random or systematic, the uncertainties on a result should remain in their original category regardless of how that result is subsequently used. The two categories should be kept separate in the progressive combination of uncertainties throughout a complex experiment, in the statement of the final result of that experiment, and when using that result in any further experiments. Finally it is recommended that randomization techniques be introduced wherever practicable into experimental procedures in order to reduce the systematic uncertainties.

Section 2

Random uncertainties

The uncertainties that come under this heading are those that have been derived by statistical methods from a number of repeated readings. However the total random uncertainty on the final result of an experiment may not be due entirely to random fluctuations of measurements made during that experiment. Contributions to the total random uncertainty may also arise from quantities that are constant during that experiment, as the values of these quantities themselves will usually have been derived from repeated measurements from which an estimate of the uncertainty due to random effects was obtained. The calibration factor of an instrument is clearly an example of a parameter that will be constant throughout an experiment but which nevertheless has an uncertainty in its numerical value due to random causes.

Strictly, at some stage in the analysis of the results of repeated measurements it is necessary to show that they are consistent with the Normal or, in certain circumstances, some other distribution. However, mathematical tests for Normality are only satisfactory if there are more than about 30 observations, see Appendix 3. For fewer observations the Normal distribution must be assumed, but, under these circumstances, it is good practice to examine the data visually. The justification for assuming that the distribution is Normal is that this has been found to be so for most cases in which observations have been examined in detail, as indeed predicted by the Central Limit theorem. Nevertheless it should be recognized that this is an assumption which may not always be justified. In the rest of this booklet, except where explicitly stated, the discussion of random uncertainties will be restricted to those cases where the underlying distribution is Normal.

Assessment

If the measured value of a quantity is represented by a parameter y, then, for a Normal distribution, the probability of y having a value lying between y and $y+dy$ is given by:

$$P(y)\,dy = \frac{1}{\sigma\sqrt{2\pi}}\exp\left[-\frac{(y-\mu)^2}{2\sigma^2}\right]dy$$

where μ is a constant equal to the value of y at the maximum of the curve, and σ is a measure of the dispersion or width of the curve; the quantity σ^2 is called the variance of the distribution. As will be shown below σ can be estimated from an analysis of the observations and this estimate together with the number of degrees of freedom (see page 9) are used to derive the random uncertainty.

If a sample of n measurements $y_1, y_2 \ldots y_n$ is taken, it can be shown that the best estimate of the constant μ of the distribution is given by the MEAN VALUE $\bar{y}$ of the sample, where

$$\bar{y} = \frac{1}{n} \sum_{i=1}^{n} y_i \qquad [2.1]$$

and the best estimate of the variance σ^2 of the distribution is given by the VARIANCE $S^2(y)$ of the sample, where

$$S^2(y) = \frac{1}{n-1} \sum_{i=1}^{n} (y_i - \bar{y})^2 \ . \qquad [2.2]$$

The quantity $S(y)$ is called the STANDARD DEVIATION of the sample and $\sum_{i=1}^{n} (y_i - \bar{y})^2$ is called the RESIDUAL SUM OF SQUARES.

Because any mean value $\bar{y}$ is derived from a limited number of measurements n, repeat determinations of $\bar{y}$ will produce a series of different values. For large values of n, the Central Limit theorem states that these values of $\bar{y}$ will lie on a distribution that is close to Normal irrespective of the distribution of $y*$. The standard deviation of this distribution could of course be obtained from a number of determinations of $\bar{y}$, but alternatively it can be estimated from the dispersion of measurements in a single mean value. This estimate is called the STANDARD ERROR OF THE MEAN, (SEOM), $S(\bar{y})$ and is given by:

$$S^2(\bar{y}) = \frac{1}{n(n-1)} \sum_{i=1}^{n} (y_i - \bar{y})^2$$
$$= \frac{S^2(y)}{n} \qquad [2.3]$$

---

* In more sophisticated forms the Central Limit theorem states that the folding together of a large number of distributions of independent size and shape will tend to the Normal distribution provided that the individual variances are finite and that these variances are of the same order of magnitude, i.e. no one distribution dominates the others.

and $S^2(\bar{y})$ is called the VARIANCE OF THE MEAN. Note that the standard deviation depends only on the precision of the technique and apparatus used and, so long as these are not changed, it will not change significantly however many observations are taken; on the other hand, the standard error of the mean depends on the number of observations in the sample as well as on the precision of the technique. The two quantities therefore present different information and the statement of both in a result may sometimes be appropriate.

In some circumstances the expected distribution may be other than Normal, for example binomial. Provided that the observations are found to agree with the expected distribution, the type of distribution should be stated together with sufficient parameters to define the distribution quantitatively. In other circumstances the frequency distribution may not even approximate to the expected distribution and in such cases it is essential to see if there is any trend or correlation which may be extracted from the data. In such distributions where no correlation can be found, the frequency distribution should be quoted in graphical or other convenient form and under these circumstances no contribution should accrue to the random category from this cause but due allowance must be made in the systematic category.

Grouped data

There are circumstances when measurements of a given physical quantity are taken in groups rather than as a single consecutive series. This is sometimes done for convenience, but often it is a deliberate attempt to randomize certain systematic effects by, for instance, repeating the setting-up procedure before each group of measurements, or carrying them out on different days in possibly different ambient conditions.

Before the readings from these groups are combined they should be tested to see whether the dispersion of the mean values of the groups is consistent with the dispersion of the readings in the individual groups. There are three possibilities. Case A: the mean values and the dispersions are all self-consistent. Case B: the dispersion of the mean values of the groups is consistent with the dispersions of the individual measurements within groups, although the latter dispersions differ significantly from each other, i.e. some groups consist of more precise measurements than other groups. Case C: the mean values of the groups differ from each other by more than would be expected from the dispersion of the measurements.

The method of combining the data from the groups differs for each of the three cases, and this is described in Appendix 4.

Experiments involving measurements of several physical quantities

While many experiments consist of observations on only a single physical quantity others may involve several quantities. In order to make an assessment of the random uncertainty on the final result it is first necessary to determine its variance from the observed variances on the separate measurements involved. If the value Y, of a physical quantity is determined by a combination of independent measurements $a, b, c, \ldots$ of separate physical quantities by the relationship $Y = f(a, b, c, \ldots)$, and the estimated variances on $a, b, c \ldots$ are $S^2(a), S^2(b), S^2(c) \ldots$ respectively, then the estimated variance on Y, $S^2(Y)$ is given by

$$S^2(Y) = \left(\frac{\partial Y}{\partial a}\right)^2 S^2(a) + \left(\frac{\partial Y}{\partial b}\right)^2 S^2(b) + \left(\frac{\partial Y}{\partial c}\right)^2 S^2(c) \ldots \qquad [2.4]$$

Also, for $\bar{Y} = f(\bar{a}, \bar{b}, \bar{c} \ldots)$, a similar formula holds for the variance of the mean $S^2(\bar{Y})$ in terms of the variances of the individual means $S^2(\bar{a})$, $S^2(\bar{b})$, $S^2(\bar{c}) \ldots$ and is

$$S^2(\bar{Y}) = \left(\frac{\partial \bar{Y}}{\partial \bar{a}}\right)^2 S^2(\bar{a}) + \left(\frac{\partial \bar{Y}}{\partial \bar{b}}\right)^2 S^2(\bar{b}) + \left(\frac{\partial \bar{Y}}{\partial \bar{c}}\right)^2 S^2(\bar{c}) \ldots \qquad [2.5]$$

$$= \sum_i \alpha_i$$

where

$$\alpha_{\bar{a}} = \left(\frac{\partial \bar{Y}}{\partial \bar{a}}\right)^2 S^2(\bar{a}) \text{ etc., and } i = \bar{a}, \bar{b}, \bar{c}, \text{ etc.}$$

Although the parameters $a, b, c \ldots$ have here been taken as actual measurements, in a typical experiment they may also include correction factors and physical constants.

In addition to neglecting higher order terms, these equations assume that all the component uncertainties are independent of each other. This is usually the case, but there are occasions when this is not so. A simple example may make this clear.

Suppose that the measurement Y depends on a reading r_1 of an instrument and the instrument's calibration factor c, i.e. $Y = f(cr_1)$, then the variances of r_1 and c are independent and both contribute to the variance of Y. If however the measurement Y depends on the ratio of readings r_1/r_2 from the same instrument, and the calibration factor c is the same for both readings, i.e. $Y = f(cr_1/cr_2)$, then, because the value of Y is independent of c, the variance of Y is also independent of the variance on c. This example is trivial but shows the need to express equations in their basic components to ensure that they are all independent. For methods of dealing with partially correlated components the reader should refer to textbooks on statistics.

Using equations 2.4 or 2.5 a value can then be calculated for the variance, and hence the standard error of the mean, of the final quantity. However, in order for this variance to be of use, for example, in comparing one result with another, it is necessary to know the number of degrees of freedom.

Degrees of freedom

This is the number of independent terms in the residual sum of squares and is usually denoted by v. For a straight mean of n observations it is $(n-1)$, for a least squares fit to a straight line it would be $(n-2)$, while for certain applications of the F test it is $(n-r)$ where the n observations are grouped into r sets.

Although there is no physical meaning to the number of degrees of freedom in the variance of the value of a quantity which has been derived from measurements of separate quantities, it is possible to estimate the 'effective number of degrees of freedom' v_{eff}, in $S^2(\bar{Y})$ by the use of the following approximate formula (see ASPIN, A. A. *Biometrika*, 1949, **36**, 290 and WELCH, B. L. *Biometrika*, 1947, **34**, 28).

$$\frac{1}{v_{eff}} = \frac{\sum_i \alpha_i^2 / v_i}{\left(\sum_i \alpha_i\right)^2} = \sum_i c_i^2 / v_i \qquad [2.6]$$

where $c_i = \alpha_i / \sum_i \alpha_i$ and α_i is defined in equation 2.5. Thus c_i is the fractional contribution of the ith component to the total random uncertainty, and v_i is the number of degrees of freedom associated with this component. In general equation 2.6 will yield a non-integer number which should be rounded downwards to the next integral number. It must be emphasized that equation 2.6 is only an approximation and becomes less valid when the components have small numbers of degrees of freedom. A further discussion appears in Appendix 2.

In stating v_{eff} for the final result it is, in principle, also necessary to state the number of degrees of freedom associated with each component in order that subsequent significance tests may be correctly made. However v_{eff} is mainly determined by the component having the largest value of the quantity c_i^2 / v_i and it is shown in Appendix 2 that minor components have, in many cases, very little influence on v_{eff}. Thus for many practical situations it is unnecessary to quote the number of degrees of freedom for minor components although it should be borne in mind that circumstances can arise in which a detailed statement is desirable. The component having the largest value of the quantity c_i^2 / v_i is usually the result of the dispersion of the experimenter's own measurements, but it is just

9

conceivable, for example, that the largest value may come from some prior measurement of a constant. In such cases it would obviously be necessary to quote the number of degrees of freedom for both components. If the number of degrees of freedom is so great that for all practical purposes it can be considered infinite then it is sufficient to indicate that the number is large.

Confidence limits

From a knowledge of the SEOM it is possible to predict the likely result of a repeated set of measurements, by giving the probability, P, that the result will lie between $\bar{y}+\delta_1$ and $\bar{y}-\delta_2$, where $\bar{y}$ is the sample mean. The quantities $\bar{y}+\delta_1$, $\bar{y}-\delta_2$ are called the upper and lower CONFIDENCE LIMITS respectively, the interval $\delta_1+\delta_2$ is called the CONFIDENCE INTERVAL and P is called the CONFIDENCE LEVEL. For a Normal distribution the confidence interval is symmetrical about the mean value $\bar{y}$ and it is only necessary to calculate δ_1 using the formula:

$$\delta_1 = t \times (\text{SEOM}) \qquad [2.7]$$

where the value of t (often called Student's t) appropriate to the confidence level required and the number of degrees of freedom, can be obtained from Table 3. From this table it can be seen that the common practice of equating three times the SEOM with the value of the 99% confidence limits is in serious error for fewer than about 8 degrees of freedom and indeed is marginally wrong for large numbers of degrees of freedom.

Significance tests

The results of an experiment often have to be compared with those obtained from one or more similar experiments. When carrying out such a comparison one criterion that can be used is whether the results differ by more than would have been expected from the effect of the random fluctuations observed during the experiments; some statistical significance tests for doing this are given in Appendix 3.

In these tests a parameter is calculated which involves, among other quantities, the random uncertainty of the mean value of each of the measurements. However the random uncertainty of a measurement required for these tests is not necessarily the total random uncertainty that has been derived according to the criteria and procedures discussed in this Code. The only component uncertainties that should be included in these significance tests are those associated with physical causes that have influenced each experiment independently. All quantities measured during separate experiments are obviously independent, while physical

10

constants common to these experiments are not independent and thus the random uncertainties associated with these constants would be excluded from the significance tests. On the other hand, if the experiments are carried out by different methods involving different physical constants their random uncertainties must then be included in the significance tests.

When stating the random uncertainty of a result it is quite obviously impossible to foresee the future experiments with which the result will be compared. For this reason it is recommended that the individual random uncertainties associated with the various component physical quantities involved are listed in full so that those appropriate to a subsequent significance test may be selected.

The statement of random uncertainty

The random uncertainty may be expressed as the SEOM or as confidence limits expressed as the 95% or 99% or some other confidence level. Of course, since the number of degrees of freedom should also be quoted it is always possible to change from one expression for the random uncertainty to another by the use of the t factor (Table 3). However in choosing the appropriate confidence level the following considerations should be noted. In those cases in which the fluctuation of readings due to random effects have been studied experimentally for large numbers of observations, it has been found that, while the Normal distribution is followed fairly closely out to about the 95% level, there are considerably more readings outside the 99% confidence limits than predicted by this distribution. There is of course no reason for experimental observations to follow the Normal distribution exactly – it is a convenient mathematical expression which fits most of the experimental observations, as indeed predicted by the Central Limit theorem. Clearly the uncertainty may be underestimated if the Normal distribution is used to predict the 99% level. On the other hand systematic uncertainties are frequently estimated as being 'not more than $\pm x\%$' and, although this is not claimed to be the exact equivalent of a 99% confidence level, combining such systematic uncertainties with the random uncertainties estimated at the 99% confidence level is clearly better than combining them with the standard error of the mean. Although the practice of combining random uncertainties with systematic uncertainties is not recommended, the fact that the 99% confidence limits of the random uncertainties are likely to be underestimated is not really important in view of the rather subjective assessment of systematic uncertainties.

There is evidently no overwhelming reason why one method of presenting random uncertainties should always be used rather than another, nor is there any customary usage in the matter. Nevertheless, when applying significance tests it is the standard error of the mean and the number of degrees of freedom that are required, and in an attempt to achieve some measure of uniformity this Code of Practice suggests that the random uncertainty should be stated in terms of these two parameters.

Conclusions

The component random uncertainties that go to make up the total random uncertainty on the result of an experiment should include not only those derived from measurements carried out during the course of that experiment, but also the random uncertainties associated with any constants, calibration factors and previous measurements that are utilized. A full discussion of accuracy should include a list of all these components in order that a proper selection may be made for significance tests. In principle it is also necessary to give the number of degrees of freedom associated with each component, but in practice it will often be sufficient to give only those associated with the main components that affect the degrees of freedom on the final result, or to state that the number of degrees of freedom is large, i.e. effectively infinite. It is recommended that the total random uncertainty should be stated in the form of the standard error of the mean together with its effective degrees of freedom. Combination with the systematic uncertainty to give the overall uncertainty is deprecated, but if this is required for some special reason, then the combination should be made with the random uncertainty in the form of the 99% confidence limits. For any random uncertainties that are based on non-Normal distributions the form of the distribution should be described graphically or by some other suitable method.

Section 3

Systematic uncertainties

As discussed in Section 1, the systematic uncertainty of a measurement, in the convention adopted in this Code, is that component of the uncertainty which is estimated by considering the physical effects expected to influence the result and, in those cases where repeated measurements do not follow a Normal or other appropriate law, from an assessment of the observed distribution. The first step in the estimation of this uncertainty is for the experimenter to identify those aspects of the measurement that can affect its value; the second step is to allocate uncertainty limits to allow for each of these effects. Successful identification of such effects depends very much on the experience and judgment (and even perhaps intuition) of the experimenter. Some effects are easily identified, for example the possible systematic inaccuracy of an instrument calibration factor, or the inequality of two parts of an instrument whose accuracy depends on their equality. However, an effect may remain quite unsuspected until the result is redetermined by an experiment utilizing some completely different principle. The reasons for the results of independent experiments differing by more than their estimated overall uncertainty limits are as often due to overlooking effects that influence the results as to underestimating those that are known.

Whereas in the treatment of random uncertainties a straightforward statistical procedure can be applied, for systematic uncertainties, in contrast, it is not possible to express the uncertainty in terms of a confidence level and confidence interval, since the probability distribution is not known. Thus it is recommended that the component systematic uncertainties be stated as overall limits, and no attempt should be made to express them in forms which imply a detailed knowledge of the distribution, for example as a standard deviation. These overall limits may be derived from subsidiary experiments or theoretical considerations. Whenever possible an experiment should be designed to reveal the causes of systematic uncertainties by varying as many as possible of the conditions under which the experiment is carried out. From the variations in the results so produced it is sometimes possible to see their cause and either eliminate them or apply further correction factors. In other cases no such solution comes to light but it may be possible to vary the conditions sufficiently to be able to apply statistical methods to the results;

this is known as randomizing the conditions. In the last resort there are likely to remain cases where neither of these courses is successful and an estimation of the uncertainty must be made based on the experimenter's assessment of the situation. Experience in many different fields of science has shown that there is a strong tendency to underestimate the magnitude of systematic uncertainties. It is important therefore to consider all possible components of the systematic uncertainty and to assign realistic values to them.

A difficulty arises when the uncertainties are judged to be asymmetrically placed around the most likely value of a quantity. Suppose a calibration factor is stated to be 1.35 units with a systematic uncertainty of ±0.04 units. All that is implied by this statement is that the value of the calibration factor is likely to lie within the range 1.31 to 1.39 units, although many experimenters would feel that it is more likely to be nearer 1.35 units than the extremes of the range. In some cases however a physical effect may be thought to bias a result in one direction only, for example, the heat loss in an experiment on thermal conductivity where the temperatures are such that no heat gain could possibly occur. The experimenter may estimate that the maximum possible correction for this effect would be +0.6%, but since he is so careful about the precautions taken he is reasonably confident that any loss that takes place is negligible. He therefore states that the correction factor to allow for this effect is 1.000 (−0.000, +0.006). It would obviously be incorrect to state this as 1.000 ± 0.003. Nevertheless it should be realized that there is an element of inconsistency in what has been done. If he is really confident about the efficacy of the precautions taken then he should state that the uncertainty is considered to be negligible. On the other hand, if he does think that there may indeed be a heat loss necessitating a correction of not more than 0.6%, then it might be more appropriate to apply a correction factor half way between the two uncertainty limits, i.e. 1.003 ± 0.003. There is no hard and fast rule in this matter, and there may well be occasions when it is correct to give asymmetrical uncertainties about a correction factor. There are, of course, cases when symmetrical uncertainties around a component correction factor become asymmetrical in the final result because of some mathematical operation, e.g. a power law relationship.

One result of categorizing uncertainties by the method of their estimation is that there will be circumstances when a systematic uncertainty will be allocated to allow for a variable effect. This may occur for instance if measurements are found to exhibit a bimodal distribution when a Normal distribution would have been expected, and supplementary experiments and theoretical investigations have failed to trace the cause of these variations. As they do not follow the Normal distribution, it is not permissible to calculate confidence limits from the data and all that can

14

be done is to use experience and judgment and take into account the range of measurements in order to allocate limits to this systematic uncertainty.

Experiments involving measurements of several physical quantities

If the value Y of a physical quantity depends on a number of measurements a, b, c ... of separate physical quantities by the relation

$$Y = f(a, b, c \ldots),$$

then, if the measurements are all independent, the component of the systematic uncertainty $(\Delta Y)_a$ associated with Y due to the systematic uncertainty Δa on the measurement a is given by

$$(\Delta Y)_a = \left| \frac{\partial Y}{\partial a} \right| \Delta a \quad . \tag{3.1}$$

There is no rigorous method of combining these components to give the overall systematic uncertainty ΔY. There are two methods that have been used in practice. The first combines them by arithmetic addition:

$$\Delta Y = (\Delta Y)_a + (\Delta Y)_b + (\Delta Y)_c + \ldots$$

$$= \left| \frac{\partial Y}{\partial a} \right| \Delta a + \left| \frac{\partial Y}{\partial b} \right| \Delta b + \left| \frac{\partial Y}{\partial c} \right| \Delta c + \ldots \tag{3.2}$$

The second method combines them in quadrature i.e.

$$(\Delta Y)^2 = (\Delta Y)_a^2 + (\Delta Y)_b^2 + (\Delta Y)_c^2 + \ldots$$

$$= \left(\frac{\partial Y}{\partial a} \right)^2 (\Delta a)^2 + \left(\frac{\partial Y}{\partial b} \right)^2 (\Delta b)^2 + \left(\frac{\partial Y}{\partial c} \right)^2 (\Delta c)^2 + \ldots \tag{3.3}$$

The first method is likely to overestimate the size of the total systematic uncertainty and can be considered as an estimate of the maximum possible limit. The second method tends to underestimate the total systematic uncertainty particularly when one of the components is considerably larger than the others. For an extension of this method and a discussion of the underlying assumptions see WAGNER, S. *PTB Mitteilungen*, 1969, **79**, 343,* who discusses the case in which systematic uncertainties have rectangular probability distributions.

Although the parameters a, b, c ... have been here taken to be actual measurements, in a typical experiment they will also include correction

---

* An English version is available from the Physikalisch-Technische Bundesanstalt, Braunschweig, as report number FMRB 31/69.

factors and physical constants. If any such parameters have component systematic uncertainties they will all contribute to the systematic uncertainty on Y, and should be combined by using equation 3.2 or 3.3 as before.

In stating the systematic uncertainty of a physical quantity the component parts should be listed, together with the actual value of any constants and correction factors used; the method of summing the component parts should also be indicated. In reporting measurements of the highest accuracy it will of course be necessary for the experimenter to justify as far as possible his estimates of the component systematic uncertainties. In other situations, such as in short reports etc., this will be impracticable although an experimenter must be able to produce such a justification if challenged.

The choice of method for the combination of systematic uncertainties where some or all are asymmetrical is difficult. Clearly all uncertainties having the same sign, including the symmetrical ones, can be summed linearly to obtain separate positive and negative uncertainties. Alternatively the uncertainties (of the same sign) may be summed in quadrature but the justification for this procedure is even more tenuous than for the analogous case for symmetrical uncertainties.

Conclusions

An attempt should be made to examine every component part of an experiment that could affect the result, and individual uncertainty limits should be allocated to express the largest effect that each component may have on the final result. These estimated component systematic uncertainties should be stated as overall limits and not in a form (such as a standard deviation) that implies knowledge of a probability distribution. In a full discussion of the accuracy of an experiment, the component systematic uncertainties should be listed together with the values of the constants or correction factors with which they are associated. An estimate of the total systematic uncertainty should be stated together with its method of derivation from its components.

Section 4

Statement of the final result

In stating the uncertainty of the final result the degree of detail that is given will depend not only on the amount of information available, but also on the context in which the result is quoted. Scientific articles reporting experimental work of primary importance, such as the measurement of physical constants or comparisons of national standards, require a comprehensive discussion and statement of the uncertainties involved in order that meaningful comparisons may be made with other results. On the other hand certain routine measurements may require only a brief statement of uncertainty; each experimenter must decide for himself how much detail is appropriate in the circumstances. Even so the statement must not be ambiguous.

Mean value and associated uncertainties

Usually the final result will be derived from a series of measurements of one or more physical quantities, together with the application of appropriate correction factors. Unless otherwise indicated it is to be assumed that a series of measurements on the same quantity has been combined by taking the arithmetic mean; the use of any other method should be stated and justified.

As noted previously, there are several ways in which the random uncertainty may be quoted; however the parameters required for the application of significance tests are the SEOM and the number of degrees of freedom and hence it is recommended that the random uncertainty be quoted in terms of these. The systematic uncertainty should be quoted as the experimenter's estimate of the total systematic uncertainty.

For all except the briefest statement of accuracy it is recommended that the random and systematic uncertainties be quoted separately, for reasons that have been discussed earlier. In this way useful information contained in the statement of random uncertainties is not discarded by combining them with systematic uncertainties which, it must be emphasized, are quite different estimates. It is of course always open to the user of an accuracy statement to combine the two categories in any way he wishes, for example, by combining the systematic uncertainty with the 99 % confidence limit of the random uncertainty either by taking their arithmetic sum or the square root of the sum of the squares; however the combination of a systematic uncertainty with the standard error of the mean would be quite wrong. Alternatively a method (WAGNER, S. PTB report number FMRB 31/69) in which the systematic uncertainties are assumed to have rectangular probability distributions could be used. So far as is known no experimental verification has been undertaken to show that this or any other method of handling systematic uncertainties does in fact lead to a realistic assessment of the combined uncertainties.

Another general recommendation is that, in order to avoid ambiguity, the statement of accuracy should be made in sentence form rather than in an abbreviated notation. The following are some examples of acceptable statements for different types of situations.* The nomenclature used is that adopted in this Code but it should be obvious how these statements can be reworded to conform to other schools of thought (see Appendix 1).

In reporting the final result of an experiment requiring a comprehensive statement of accuracy the following form could be used:

'The mean corrected result was 1.036 cm^2 g^{-1} *having a standard error of the mean of* 0.002 cm^2 g^{-1} *with 5 degrees of freedom; the total systematic uncertainty was estimated to be* ±0.025 cm^2 g^{-1}*.'*

This should be accompanied by two lists giving details of all the components that have contributed to the two uncertainties together with the degrees of freedom of the random components; this is so that an appropriate selection may be made when applying significance tests, and also in order that adjustments can subsequently be made should better values for constants become available. The method used to combine the systematic uncertainties should also be stated.

In simpler statements of accuracy the list of component uncertainties will often be abbreviated or even omitted. In the case of certain routine calibrations of instruments the standard deviation of the calibration procedure may be known from previous calibrations of similar instruments. Provided that the measurements on the instrument under calibration are shown to be consistent with previous results a statement may be made in the following terms:

'The SEOM *of this calibration factor is unlikely to exceed* 1.0%, *this being*

---

* Further discussions on the methods of deriving and stating uncertainties may be found in a collection of papers published as *Precision Measurements and Calibration* National Bureau of Standards Special Publication 300, Vol 1, 1969, US Government Printing Office, Washington DC, USA.

based on experience with a large number of calibrations of similar instruments. The total systematic uncertainty is estimated to be ±0.5%.'

It is important that whenever the random or systematic uncertainty is considered to be negligible this should be stated explicitly rather than omitting the statement. In some routine reports it may not be necessary or desirable to quote any uncertainty at all but again, to avoid ambiguity, a statement should make the situation clear. For example:

'The frequency was 5791 Hz, all uncertainties being negligible to this degree of rounding.'

This type of statement implies that any uncertainty is small compared to $\pm\frac{1}{2}$ unit in the last significant figure given.

It is seen therefore that the Code of Practice does not necessarily imply that a comprehensive statement of uncertainties should be given under all circumstances; what is important is that a statement of uncertainty should be made in an unambiguous way. Statements such as an unqualified '3.8 ± 0.2 cm', or 'the accuracy is ±0.02 g' or that 'the precision was ±0.1 %' are not only meaningless but can be misleading. The absence of a statement is itself ambiguous.

Rounding

When processing data in the course of an experiment it is often necessary to round numbers to fewer significant figures; for example, it is only in exceptional cases that all the digits displayed on a calculating machine as the result of a division would be noted down. There are two stages in rounding, first the decision as to the appropriate number of significant figures, and then the actual method of rounding. The latter will be dealt with first.

Method of rounding

It is recommended that rounding should be taken to unity in the last significant place retained, but if in exceptional cases a rounding interval of 2 or 5 units is felt to be appropriate then the fineness of rounding must be stated. Mean values should be rounded according to the following rules:

(a) Round to the nearest figure, e.g. 2.364 rounds to 2.36, whereas 2.366 rounds to 2.37.

(b) When the figures to be discarded fall midway between alternatives round to the nearest even number, hence 2.365 rounds downwards to

2.36 whereas 2.375 rounds upwards to 2.38.*

(c) When discarding several digits, this should be done in one operation, e.g. 2.346 rounds to 2.3 in one operation whereas in two stages it would have been rounded to 2.35 and then to 2.4.

When rounding standard errors and other uncertainties, rounding should always be upwards towards a more pessimistic estimate of accuracy, e.g. a standard error of 0.02332 units would be rounded to 0.024 units to two significant figures and to 0.03 units to one significant figure. On the other hand the effective number of degrees of freedom should be rounded downwards to the next integer. When confidence limits are stated they should be calculated from the unrounded values of the SEOM.

Degree of rounding

When recording instrument readings the number of significant figures is usually determined by the limit of estimation of the instrument. In any subsequent calculations it is recommended that sufficient additional figures should be carried through to avoid the possibility of loss of accuracy due to excessive rounding.

It is usually in the statement of the final result that the real decision has to be taken about the degree of rounding. It can be claimed that the statement of a result such as 2.36285 kg with a standard error of the mean of 0.00233 kg (5 degrees of freedom) is acceptable because the size of the uncertainty guards against undue reliance being placed on the significance of the last digits of the mean value. However, normal practice would be to round both the mean value and the uncertainty to fewer significant figures. A number of schemes have been devised from which the degree of rounding appropriate to the accuracy of the result can be estimated. These usually rely on the standard deviation of the standard error, $S(\bar{y})/\sqrt{2v}$, where v is the number of degrees of freedom in the standard error of the mean $S(\bar{y})$, see Section 2. It can however be shown that it requires a large number of measurements or degrees of freedom to reduce the 95% confidence limits on the estimate of the SEOM to less than $\pm 10\%$ of the SEOM, and that for fewer than 9 measurements the SEOM is estimated to no better than $+100\%$ -35% at the 95% confidence level (the limits are asymmetrical). It can be seen therefore that it is hardly

---

* For rounding intervals other than unity, when rounding to n in the last figure, and a number falls midway between alternatives, then round to the nearest $2n$, e.g. when rounding to 2 in the last digit, 2.21 rounds to 2.20 rather than 2.22, whereas 2.31 rounds to 2.32.

worth quoting the SEOM to more than two significant figures, and for few observations only one significant figure may be justified.

One can therefore formulate a simple rule of thumb that the SEOM should be rounded to no more than two significant figures and that the mean value should be rounded to unity in the last digit affected by the SEOM. Thus with only five degrees of freedom the previous result would be rounded to 2.363 kg with a SEOM of 0.003 kg. A similar criterion may be used for rounding confidence limits.

When rounding the mean value the number of significant figures should usually be based on the random rather than the systematic uncertainty. In precise experiments under good experimental conditions it is often found that the random uncertainty is far less than the systematic uncertainty. For example, the previous mean value of 2.36285 kg has unrounded 99% confidence limits of ±0.00932 kg calculated from a SEOM of 0.00233 kg and 5 degrees of freedom. Suppose that in addition the systematic uncertainty has been assessed as ±3%, i.e. ±0.07 kg. It might seem reasonable in these circumstances to round the mean to 2.36 kg or even to 2.4 kg. However, systematic uncertainties are often derived from subjective judgment and later assessment may change them. Excessive rounding can then cause loss of useful information when using significance tests to compare the result with a subsequent experiment.

One final suggestion on this topic is that for numbers much greater than unity, superfluous zeros should be avoided, e.g. if 44621 is rounded to three significant figures, i.e. 44600, this should be written as 44.6×10^3 or 4.46×10^4. It should be emphasized that significant zeros should not be omitted, e.g. if a result is rounded to 47.0 it should not be stated as just 47.

Section 5

Recommendations

The recommendations put forward in this Code of Practice are summarized together with references to the Sections in which they are discussed in greater detail.

The uncertainty on a measurement should be put into one of two categories depending on how the uncertainty is derived; a random uncertainty is derived by a statistical analysis of repeated measurements while a systematic uncertainty is estimated by non-statistical methods.
(Section 1)

When combining the uncertainties on individual measurements in a complex experiment involving measurements on several physical quantities the two categories of uncertainties should be kept separate throughout.
(Section 1)

In such an experiment the total random uncertainty should be obtained from the combination of the variances of the means of the individual measurements together with those associated with any constants, calibration factors, etc.
(Section 2)

The component systematic uncertainties should be estimated in the form of maximum values or overall limits to the uncertainties.   (Section 3)

In reporting measurements of the highest accuracy, a full statement of the result of an experiment should be in three parts, the mean corrected value, the random uncertainty and the systematic uncertainty, as follows:

(a) *Mean corrected value*
The choice of any value other than the arithmetic mean should be justified.

(b) *Random uncertainty*

(i) The standard error of the mean is the preferred presentation.

(ii) The effective number of degrees of freedom should be given, or a statement should be made to the effect that the number is large.

(iii) The components that have contributed to the final uncertainty should be listed in sufficient detail to make it clear whether they would remain constant if the experiment were repeated.   (Section 4)

(c) *Systematic uncertainty*

(i) The estimate of the total systematic uncertainty should be stated.

(ii) Each component of the systematic uncertainty should be listed, expressed as the estimated maximum value of that uncertainty.

(iii) The method used to combine these component uncertainties should be made clear.   (Section 3)

The combination of random and systematic uncertainties to give an 'overall uncertainty' is deprecated, but if in a particular case this is thought to be appropriate then it should be given in addition to the two uncertainties, together with the method of combination.   (Section 4)

Each experimenter must decide for himself how much detail is given in the statement of uncertainty. Experimental work of primary importance requires a comprehensive discussion of the uncertainties involved: routine measurements may require only a brief statement. Although there are many circumstances when a statement of uncertainty may be less than complete, care is necessary to avoid such a statement being ambiguous.   (Section 4)

The statement of uncertainty should be made in sentence form rather than an abbreviated notation.   (Section 4)

Appendix 1

Meanings of the word *error*

Reference is made in Section 1 to a division of opinion concerning the use of the word *error*. Briefly, one body of opinion regards the error as being the difference between the experimental result and the true value, whereas the other regards the error of the result as its uncertainty, i.e. the number placed after the plus and minus sign. In addition there are several other uses of the word *error*, e.g. the deviation between the measured result and the conventional true value,* or a mistake in a calculation etc. Many of these usages are built into the technical nomenclature, and this is unlikely to change. All that can be done here is to suggest that whenever the word *error* is used its meaning in that particular context should always be made clear to the reader.

Returning now to the use of the word *error* to mean either, on the one hand the difference between the measured and true values, or on the other hand the uncertainty of a result, it is interesting to note that whichever concept an author uses, the scientific paper will usually be equally intelligible to both bodies of opinion. Moreover, the actual numbers following the plus and minus signs would be the same for either school. However in discussing the concepts of errors and uncertainties it is necessary to keep to precise and clear cut definitions.

As this dichotomy of view is not widely appreciated the two concepts will be described at some length. The terminology used in this discussion is typical but it must be remembered that there are many variations of detail. Thus what is here termed the *mean corrected result*, for example, may be described by a different phrase elsewhere. Such variations are not important in this Appendix which is solely concerned with differences in the use of the word *error* and terms containing this word. For simplicity, the discussion will be confined in the first instance to just one type of error, namely that due to systematic causes.

---

* The conventional true value is defined as 'a value approximating to the true value of a quantity such that for the purposes for which that value is used the difference between the two values can be neglected'. Thus it may be a convenient term to use in connection with instrument specification but has little application in the uncertainty statements associated with measurements of the highest accuracy with which this booklet is mainly concerned.

Figure 1 represents diagrammatically the steps by which the best estimate for a quantity is obtained from experimental observations. The lower part of Figure 1 represents the school of thought which, for reasons that will become apparent, supports what will be called the true-value concept, while the upper part represents the other school of thought which supports what will be called the observables-only concept. The true value in this context means that actual value* of the quantity being measured; it is of course unknown and unknowable. Starting from the left hand side of Figure 1 both schools of thought pool the experimental observations to obtain a reading which is converted to an uncorrected result by means of conversion and/or scale factors. Correction factors are then applied to allow for all known disturbing effects giving the corrected result, or the experimenter's best estimate of the quantity being measured. However these correction factors cannot be known exactly and the residual uncertainties, suitably combined, form the final plus and minus for both schools. Thus, numerically at least, the same final result is obtained from either concept although the terminology differs. The observables-only school calls the quantity following the plus and minus sign the systematic error whereas the other school would define systematic error as the difference between the uncorrected result and the true value. It is this use of the same term, systematic error, to describe two quite different entities that distinguishes these two schools of thought and which may cause confusion. The difference between these two uses can be emphasized by considering a hypothetical situation in which the corrected result exactly coincides with the true value. The residual systematic error (i.e. the difference between the true value and the corrected result) is thus zero on the true-value concept but the systematic error has a finite value on the observables-only concept.

Figure 2 depicts the analogous case for random effects. Here the random error of the mean result is defined on the true-value concept as the difference between the mean corrected result and the limiting mean (corrected) value which in this case is the true value as there is, by definition, no systematic error.

The situation is more complicated for the general case in which there are both random and systematic effects. This is shown in Figure 3 and here, according to the true-value school, the random error of the mean value becomes the difference between the mean corrected result and the limiting mean, while the residual systematic error becomes the difference between the limiting mean corrected value and the true value, i.e. in this

---

* or the expectation value if the conditions are such that a stochastic
quantity is involved, for example in a radioactive disintegration rate
measurement.

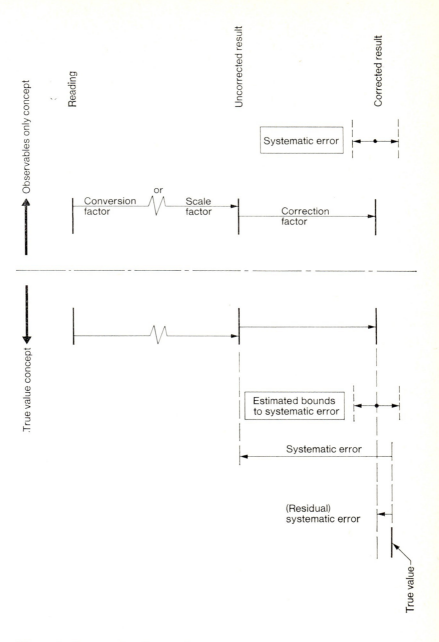

Figure 1 *Systematic effects only*

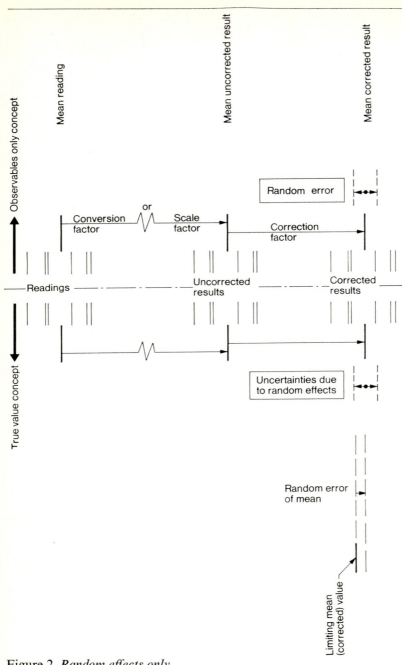

Figure 2 *Random effects only*

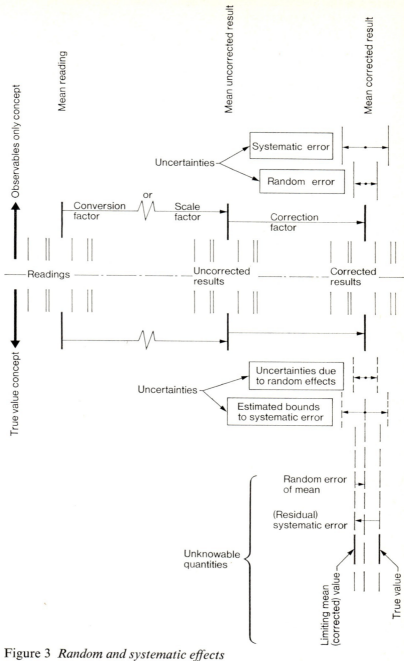

Figure 3 *Random and systematic effects*

case it is the algebraic sum of the random and residual systematic errors which is the difference between the mean corrected result and the true value.

The advantages and disadvantages of these two concepts may be briefly summarized as follows. The true-value school claims that their use of the word *error* is what might be termed the dictionary definition, and also that although the difference between the true value and the measured value can never be known exactly it is useful to have a word for this entity. Their opponents, on the other hand, claim that the adherents of the true-value school introduce the concept of true value only in order to define error, and that they never use it in any practical situation; they are thus forced into using awkward phrases such as uncertainty due to random effects and estimated bounds to the residual systematic error instead of the much more manageable phrases random error and systematic error to describe the uncertainty of a result. Further, the true-value concept becomes somewhat complicated for the general case as illustrated in Figure 3. The observables-only school also point out that it leads to a minor inconsistency since the phrase standard error of the mean is used with its conventional meaning to denote a range of values about the best estimate rather than a deviation from the true value. The simplicity of the observables-only concept is claimed by its adherents as an undoubted attraction. Obviously it is impossible to claim either concept as the right one in any absolute sense. Although the two schools differ in their nomenclature, they agree about what they are trying to do, that is to derive the best estimates of the uncertainties arising from random and systematic causes.

The purpose of this discussion, therefore, is not to press the claims of either terminology, but to point out the dangers of confusing one with the other. The practice adopted in this Code of using the word *uncertainty* wherever possible, rather than *error* has obvious advantages, and would undoubtedly be preferable were it not that the word *error* is so deeply entrenched in scientific terminology. Whether these advantages are sufficient to override the claims of established usage is a matter of opinion. While it is felt that terms such as *random uncertainty* and *systematic uncertainty* to designate both the quantity and its numerical measure, would be acceptable to most authors, some may prefer a nomenclature appropriate to one or other of the concepts described above. In this case, it will be quite clear from what has been said how the various recommendations in this Code of Practice should be re-worded.

Appendix 2

Degrees of freedom

This Code recommends that all component random uncertainties be listed and combined to give the total random uncertainty whether these components were derived during the measurement or were associated with a constant or a calibration factor. It is a relatively simple matter to calculate the effective number of degrees of freedom, v_{eff}, for such a total random uncertainty using equation 2.6 which reads:

$$\frac{1}{v_{eff}} = \frac{\sum_i \alpha_i^2 / v_i}{\left(\sum_i \alpha_i\right)^2} = \sum_i c_i^2 / v_i$$

where $c_i = \alpha_i / \sum_i \alpha_i$ and α_i is defined in equation 2.5. Thus c_i is the fraction that the ith component contributes to the total SEOM and $\sum_i c_i = 1$. If subsequently one wishes to carry out significance tests, for example Student's t test, it may be necessary to exclude some components from the total random uncertainty; this can be readily accomplished since the components should be listed, together with the number of degrees of freedom associated with the major components.

However it is instructive to consider the effect on the value of v_{eff} of the number of degrees of freedom associated with a minor component. As was pointed out in Section 2 experimental observations usually follow the Normal distribution only approximately and there is little justification in trying to distinguish between say a 95% and either a 94% or 96% confidence interval. From this it can be shown that there is no need to know t to better than $\pm 10\%$ for v_{eff} less than about 4, or to better than $\pm 5\%$ for larger values of v_{eff}. Consider the case where there are just two components, c_1 and c_2 (where c_2 is the minor component) with v_1 and v_2 degrees of freedom respectively. The following table shows the minimum integral values of v_2, which change t by less than 5% of its value for $v_2 = \infty$, for two confidence levels and for various ratios of c_1 to c_2. For larger values of v_2 the change in t is less than 5%.

Clearly in many cases the contribution of v_2 to v_{eff} can be neglected from the point of view of its influence on t.

31

v_1	Confidence level	$c_1 = 0.90$ $c_2 = 0.10$	$c_1 = 0.75$ $c_2 = 0.25$	$c_1 = 0.50$ $c_2 = 0.50$
15	95%	1	2	7
	99%	1	3	11
10	95%	1	2	7
	99%	1	3	11
5	95%	1	3	7
	99%	1	4	11

A related question is the accuracy of the value for v_{eff} given by equation 2.6 which is only an approximation. Those values of t obtained using equation 2.6 for two components and those values derived from a more accurate calculation show agreement to better than 5% for v_1 and v_2 greater than 5 and not quite such good agreement for v_1 and v_2 less than 5, see WELCH, B. L. *Biometrika* 1947, **34**, 28 and ASPIN, A. A. *Biometrika*, 1949, **36**, 290. As an example, for $v_1 = v_2 = 2$ and for the situation where the apportioning of the components leads to the worst case, viz., $c_1 = c_2$, the discrepancy amounts to 12% in the value of t. Thus equation 2.6 should be sufficiently accurate for most purposes.

Appendix 3

Tests for normality, consistency and homogeneity of data

Tests for Normality

As was mentioned in Section 2, the formulae for handling the random uncertainties strictly speaking apply only when the observations follow a Normal distribution and this should be tested before calculating confidence limits or combining them with other random uncertainties. However, it is found that these procedures for handling uncertainties are not critically dependent on the Normal distribution being followed, so long as the departure from it is not too great. Also, the Central Limit theorem indicates that non-Normal distributions tend to combine to form Normal distributions. This is fortunate for, in practice, tests for Normality require a large number of observations. For example the χ^2 test, described in A.3.1, is not very sensitive for fewer than about 30 observations. With fewer observations it is worthwhile to draw a histogram. Visual inspection may then reveal marked departures from a Normal distribution and, although it is difficult by this method to see small departures, this, as has just been pointed out, usually does not matter.

Tests for consistency and homogeneity

There are numerous statistical tests which can be applied in various circumstances but the ones most frequently used are the χ^2, t, and F tests; these are summarized in Table 1 and described in more detail below.

A.3.1 *The χ^2 test*

It can be shown that if a set of n observations is taken from a population of variance σ^2 and if the variance of the observed set is S^2, then $(n-1)S^2/\sigma^2$ for a number of sets has a distribution known as the χ^2 distribution with $(n-1)$ degree of freedom. Hence using tables for the χ^2 distribution it is possible to test whether a value of S obtained in a particular experiment, for which σ is known, is reasonable or exceptional. In general, however, σ will be unknown, but the test could be used to compare the results of particular sets of observations with the results obtained on many previous occasions assuming that the previous results give a good estimate of σ.

The χ^2 test can also be used to check whether or not a set of n observations is consistent with a Normal or indeed any other distribution, by comparing the observed frequency distribution with that expected from the assumed distribution. Suppose that a set of n observations is divided up into k classes, o_i falling into the ith class, also that from the assumed distribution the probability of an observation falling into the ith class is p_i, then the expected number in the ith class, e_i, is approximately given by np_i. However, the parameters needed to calculate p_i (e.g. the mean and the variance) are unlikely to be known from prior considerations and will therefore have to be estimated from the observations. If l such parameters are estimated in this way then it can be shown that χ^2_{obs} given by

$$\chi^2_{obs} = \sum_{i=1}^{k} (o_i - e_i)^2/e_i \qquad \text{[A.3.1.1]}$$

is approximately distributed as χ^2 with $(k-l-1)$ degrees of freedom, the approximation being reasonably valid for e_i greater than 5.

Thus by comparing the value χ^2_{obs} with the value of χ^2 from tables, at the appropriate confidence level, a decision can be made as to whether or not the agreement with the assumed distribution is reasonable. To obtain χ^2 Table 2 is entered at $N_2 = \infty$ and $N_1 = (k-l-1)$, the number of degrees of freedom in χ^2. For each value of N_1 three values of χ^2/N_1 are given corresponding to three confidence levels P, where $1-P$ is the probability of observing a value of χ^2 as large as that tabulated when the observations actually do follow the assumed distribution.

As an example consider an experiment in which the number m of β-particles emitted from a radioactive source per unit time interval is measured for a series of time intervals. Then the observed values of m should follow the Poisson distribution. The results of an experiment to test this are given in the table below. The first column gives the number of β-particles detected in equal time intervals, the second the number of intervals when that number were detected. The total number of intervals was 9995 and the total number of particles detected 48847, hence the mean number per interval is 4.89.

Assuming that the number of particles detected per unit time interval follows the Poisson distribution, the probability of detecting m particles is given by $e^{-\mu}\mu^m/m!$ where μ is the mean number of particles detected per interval. Hence the expected number of intervals when m events would be detected is $9995 \times e^{-4.89} (4.89)^m/m!$. From this expression the

34

expected number of intervals containing a given number of particles was calculated and is shown in column 3 of the table below; column 4 gives the difference between the observed and expected values. The corresponding components of χ^2, i.e. $(o-e)^2/e$, are given in column 5.

Number of particles per interval m_i	Number of intervals in which m_i particles were observed o	expected e	$o-e$	$(o-e)^2/e$
0	88	75	13	2.25
1	370	367	3	0.02
2	913	897	16	0.29
3	1457	1461	−4	0.01
4	1768	1785	−17	0.16
5	1721	1745	−24	0.33
6	1454	1421	33	0.77
7	1020	992	28	0.79
8	600	606	−6	0.06
9	308	329	−21	1.34
10	160	161	−1	0.01
11	90	72	18	4.50
12	27	29	−2	0.14
13	15	11	4	1.45
14	2	4 ⎫		
15	2	1 ⎬	−1	0.20
16	0	0 ⎭		

$$\text{Total } \chi^2 = \sum (o-e)^2/e = 12.32$$

The numbers of 14 or more β-particles per interval have been combined since, as was pointed out above, the approximations made in deriving the χ^2 test become poor when the expected number is less than about 5. There are 15 sets of data, and since the mean value has been derived from the observations, the number of degrees of freedom, which corresponds to $k-l-1$ in Table 1, is therefore 13. From Table 2 with $N_1 = 13$ and $N_2 = \infty$ the predicted value of χ^2/N_1 is approximately 1.8 for $P = 0.95$, giving χ^2 (predicted) $= 23.4$; hence one can state that the observations are in good accordance with the Poisson distribution.

A.3.2 *The t test*

This is a useful test for the comparison of two means. Suppose that a set of n_1 observations leads to a mean value $\bar{y}_1$ and a standard error of the mean of $S(\bar{y}_1)$ and a second set of n_2 observations leads to $\bar{y}_2$ and $S(\bar{y}_2)$, then the *t* test can be used to verify the hypothesis that the two sets of observations come from the same population, i.e. that the observed mean values and variances are estimates of the same population mean and variance respectively.

Under this hypothesis it can be shown that the parameter

$$t_{obs} = |\bar{y}_1 - \bar{y}_2| \left\{ \frac{(n_1 + n_2 - 2) n_1 n_2}{(n_1 + n_2) [n_1(n_1 - 1) S^2(\bar{y}_1) + n_2(n_2 - 1) S^2(\bar{y}_2)]} \right\}^{\frac{1}{2}} \quad [\text{A.3.2.1}]$$

is distributed according to the *t* distribution with $n_1 + n_2 - 2$ degrees of freedom and hence the probability of obtaining a value of *t* as large as t_{obs}, if the hypothesis adopted is true, can be obtained from tables of the *t* distribution.

The column of Table 2 corresponding to $N_1 = 1$ gives values of t^2 for different values of the degrees of freedom, entered as N_2, at three confidence levels *P*, where $1 - P$ is probability of t^2 being as large as the tabulated value when the two samples are from the same population. Table 3 gives values of *t* for various values of the degrees of freedom and at four confidence levels *P*. The relevant formulae required for the test are summarized in Table 1, while expressions for the overall mean and its standard error are given by equations A.4.8a and A.4.9a in Appendix 4.

The *t* test described above is used to examine the hypothesis that the two sets of observations came from the same population. In general when comparing the results obtained by two different methods or laboratories it is unlikely that the two sets of observations will be from populations with the same variance; also the degrees of freedom might have been obtained as v_{eff} for each set. However it is still possible to test whether or not the means are significantly different using the following modified *t* test.

If the mean, standard error of the mean and effective number of degrees of freedom for the two sets of observations are $\bar{y}_1$, $S(\bar{y}_1)$, v_1 and $\bar{y}_2$, $S(\bar{y}_2)$, v_2 respectively then it can be shown that

$$t_m = \frac{|\bar{y}_1 - \bar{y}_2|}{[S^2(\bar{y}_1) + S^2(\bar{y}_2)]^{\frac{1}{2}}} \quad [\text{A.3.2.2}]$$

is approximately distributed as *t* with *v* degrees of freedom where

36

$$v = \frac{[S^2(\bar{y}_1)+S^2(\bar{y}_2)]^2}{S^4(\bar{y}_1)/v_1+S^4(\bar{y}_2)/v_2} \quad . \tag{A.3.2.3}$$

Thus to carry out this test the value of t_m^2 is compared with the value obtained from Table 2 for the required confidence level with entries $N_1 = 1$ and $N_2 = v$ as given above. The expressions for the overall mean and its standard error are given by equations A.4.11a and A.4.13a in Appendix 4.

As an example of the first method of using the t test consider the results of an experiment carried out to compare measurements of the temperature of a body obtained by two observers using the same optical pyrometer. Each observer took ten measurements of the temperature and the results are given in the table below. The t test will be used to see whether or not there is any significant difference in the results from the two observers.

Measured temperature (°C)

Observer A	Observer B
1912	1914
1911	1913
1910	1910
1909	1910
1909	1912
1911	1914
1911	1910
1913	1912
1906	1918
1916	1914
Mean 1910.8 ± 0.84	Mean 1912.7 ± 0.78

(The uncertainties quoted are the standard errors of the mean).

In order to carry out the t test it is necessary to calculate the following quantities

$$S^2 = \frac{1}{n_1+n_2-2} \{n_1(n_1-1)S^2(\bar{y}_1)+n_2(n_2-1)S^2(\bar{y}_2)\} \tag{A.3.2.4}$$

and

$$t^2 = \frac{n_1 n_2}{n_1+n_2} \frac{(\bar{y}_1-\bar{y}_2)^2}{S^2} \quad . \tag{A.3.2.5}$$

Hence for these measurements

$$S^2 = \frac{1}{18}\{10 \times 9 \times (0.84)^2 + 10 \times 9 \times (0.78)^2\} = 6.6$$

and

$$t^2 = \frac{10 \times 10}{20} \cdot \frac{(1.9)^2}{6.6} = 2.73 \quad .$$

From Table 2, with $N_1 = 1$, $N_2 = 18$ and $P = 0.95$, t^2 is found to be 4.4. Since this is larger than the experimental value, viz., 2.73, one concludes that such a difference in the mean could arise by chance considerably more often than once in twenty times and therefore on the basis of this data it is unlikely that there is any significant difference between the results obtained by the two observers.

A.3.3 *The F test*

If S_1^2, with v_1 degrees of freedom, and S_2^2, with v_2 degrees of freedom, are two independent assessments of the variance σ^2 of a population then it can be shown that parameter $F_{obs} = S_1^2/S_2^2$ follows the F distribution. Thus by comparing the value of F_{obs} with the tabulated value of F a decision can be made on whether or not two measured variances differ significantly. The parameter F is defined to be always greater than unity, i.e. the larger estimate of the variance is taken as S_1^2. To obtain F Table 2 is entered at $N_1 = v_1$ and $N_2 = v_2$. At each entry three values of F are given corresponding to three confidence levels P, where $1 - P$ is the probability of observing a value of F as large as the tabulated value when the variances are estimates of the variance of the same population.

The F test can be extended to test the homogeneity of different sets of data. Suppose that a series of n observations fall naturally into r separate sets, the jth set containing n_j observations with mean $\bar{y}_j$ where

$$\bar{y}_j = \frac{\sum\limits_{i=1}^{n_j} w_{ij} y_{ij}}{\sum\limits_{i=1}^{n_j} w_{ij}}$$

and w_{ij} is the weight appropriate to each reading. The r sets may correspond to repeat readings made on different days. Then the F test can be used to check whether the variation within the sets is different from the variation between the sets by calculating an estimate S_1 of the standard error of the overall mean based on the variations within the sets and an estimate S_2 based on the variation between sets.

38

The residual sum of squares due to variations within the sets is

$$\sum_{j=1}^{r} \sum_{i=1}^{n_j} w_{ij}(y_{ij}-\bar{y}_j)^2$$

hence

$$S_1^2 = \frac{\sum\limits_{j=1}^{r} \sum\limits_{i=1}^{n_j} w_{ij}(y_{ij}-\bar{y}_j)^2}{(n-r)\sum\limits_{j=1}^{r} \sum\limits_{i=1}^{n_j} w_{ij}} \qquad [A.3.3.1]$$

since there are $n-r$ independent terms in the residual sum of squares. Also S_2 can be calculated from the mean values of each set using

$$S_2^2 = \frac{\sum\limits_{j=1}^{r} \sum\limits_{i=1}^{n_j} w_{ij}(\bar{y}_j-\bar{y})^2}{(r-1)\sum\limits_{j=1}^{r} \sum\limits_{i=1}^{n_j} w_{ij}} \qquad [A.3.3.2]$$

where

$$\bar{y} = \frac{\sum\limits_{j=1}^{r} \sum\limits_{i=1}^{n_j} w_{ij}y_{ij}}{\sum\limits_{j=1}^{r} \sum\limits_{i=1}^{n_j} w_{ij}} \, . \qquad [A.3.3.3]$$

The values of the weights w_{ij} are chosen so that more weight is given to the readings of high precision. If the weights are chosen so that the variance of $\bar{y}$ is a minimum then it can be shown that $w_{ij} = s^2/\sigma_{ij}^2$ where σ_{ij}^2 is the variance of the population from which y_{ij} was taken and s^2 is a constant of proportionality or normalization. In general the σ_{ij}^2 are not known and have to be estimated from the data. The following two examples cover the cases that most frequently occur in practice.

Case A All the readings y_{ij} are made to the same precision; this implies that the variances of each set of readings, viz.,

$$S^2(y_j) = \sum_{i=1}^{n_j} (y_{ij}-\bar{y}_j)^2/(n_j-1)$$

are not significantly different and this can be tested using the F test. In this case each reading is given the same weight and therefore

$$S_1^2 = \frac{\sum\limits_{j=1}^{r} \sum\limits_{i=1}^{n_j} (y_{ij}-\bar{y}_j)^2}{n(n-r)} \qquad [A.3.3.4]$$

and

$$S_2^2 = \frac{\sum\limits_{j=1}^{r} n_j(\bar{y}_j - \bar{y})^2}{n(r-1)}$$

[A.3.3.5]

where

$$\bar{y} = \frac{1}{n} \sum_{j=1}^{r} n_j \bar{y}_j \quad .$$

[A.3.3.6]

Then

$$F = \frac{S_1^2}{S_2^2} = \frac{\dfrac{1}{n-r} \sum\limits_{j=1}^{r} \sum\limits_{i=1}^{n_j} (y_{ij} - \bar{y}_j)^2}{\dfrac{1}{r-1} \sum\limits_{j=1}^{r} n_j(\bar{y}_j - \bar{y})^2}$$

[A.3.3.7]

with $(n-r)$ degrees of freedom in S_1 and $(r-1)$ in S_2.

Case B The readings within a set of measurements are all made to the same precision, but the precision of each set is not the same, i.e. $\sigma_{ij}^2 = \sigma_j^2$ for all i but σ_j^2 is not the same for all j. This implies that the variances $S^2(y_j)$ are significantly different. In this case it is appropriate to take $w_{ij} = \sigma^2/S^2(y_j)$. Thus S_1^2 and S_2^2 are given by

$$S_1^2 = \frac{1}{\sum\limits_{j=1}^{r} (1/S^2(\bar{y}_j))}$$

[A.3.3.8]

$$S_2^2 = \frac{\sum\limits_{j=1}^{r} (\bar{y}_j - \bar{y})^2/S^2(\bar{y}_j)}{(r-1) \sum\limits_{j=1}^{r} (1/S^2(\bar{y}_j))}$$

[A.3.3.9]

where

$$\bar{y} = \frac{\sum\limits_{j=1}^{r} \bar{y}_j/S^2(\bar{y}_j)}{\sum\limits_{j=1}^{r} 1/S^2(\bar{y}_j)}$$

[A.3.3.10]

and

$$S^2(\bar{y}_j) = \frac{S^2(y_j)}{n_j} \quad .$$

[A.3.3.11]

Hence

$$F = \frac{r-1}{\sum\limits_{j=1}^{r} (\bar{y}_j - \bar{y})^2 / S^2(\bar{y}_j)}$$ [A.3.3.12]

with $(n-r)$ degrees of freedom in S_1 and $(r-1)$ in S_2.

In practice, when comparing the results obtained by a number of workers, the degrees of freedom in S_1 may not be known and it is often assumed to be very large and in this case $(r-1)S_2^2/S_1^2 = \sum\limits_{j=1}^{r} (\bar{y}_j - \bar{y})^2/S^2(\bar{y}_j)$ is distributed as χ^2 with $(r-1)$ degrees of freedom. Thus the observed value of $\chi^2/(r-1) = S_2^2/S_1^2$ can be compared with the value obtained from Table 2 with $N_1 = r-1$ and $N_2 = \infty$, i.e. the test is identical with the F test for an infinite number of degrees of freedom in S_1. This is often referred to as a comparison of the internal and external errors S_1 and S_2.

Note that the test is whether or not S_1^2 is significantly greater than S_2^2 and therefore S_1^2 must be the greater of the two estimates of the variance, i.e. the formula for F must be inverted if S_2^2 is greater then S_1^2. This implies that N_1 in Table 2 is the number of degrees of freedom associated with the greater estimate of variance.

As an example of the F test consider its use to check the reproducibility of a current-measuring system used in calibrating X-ray dosemeters. The current produced in an ionization chamber by a radioactive source in nominally constant geometrical conditions was measured from time to time during the calibrations. These currents, corrected to a common reference time, are given below.

| | Date of measurement | | | | | | |
	26.9.68	29.10.68	21.12.68	17.1.69	24.1.69	28.1.69	30.1.69
Current	0.21811	0.21885	0.21829	0.21765	0.21764	0.21683	0.21709
in pA	0.21786	0.21904	0.21785	0.21704	0.21745	0.21686	0.21740
	0.21741	0.21892	0.21798	0.21680	0.21685	0.21733	0.21719
	0.21839	0.21867	0.21789	0.21680	0.21760	0.21674	0.21728
	0.21791	0.21880	0.21786	0.21673	0.21721	0.21635	0.21744
		0.21870			0.21725	0.21620	0.21751
Mean	0.21794	0.21883	0.21797	0.21700	0.21733	0.21672	0.21732
SEOM	0.00016	0.00006	0.00008	0.00017	0.00012	0.00016	0.00007

The calculated values of S_1^2 and S_2^2, assuming equal weights for all readings (i.e. *Case A* above), are given in the following table.

Sum of square deviations	Degrees of freedom	Estimated variance pA^2
each mean from grand mean		
$\sum_{j=1}^{r} n_j(\bar{y}_j - \bar{y})^2 = 1.7683 \times 10^{-5}$	$(r-1) = 6$	$S_2^2 = 75.57 \times 10^{-9}$
each observation from mean of each set		
$\sum_{j=1}^{r} \sum_{i=1}^{n_j} (y_{ij} - \bar{y}_j)^2 = 2.7021 \times 10^{-6}$	$(n-r) = 32$	$S_1^2 = 2.165 \times 10^{-9}$

Therefore $F = S_2^2/S_1^2 = 34.9$.

Since the expected value of F from Table 2 with $N_1 = 6$, $N_2 = 32$ and $P = 0.999$ is 5, then only in fewer than one in a thousand times would the observed variations between sets arise due to chance. Hence either the long term stability of the equipment is poor or the methods used to check it are not reliable.

Using the same data but employing the method of weighting described in *Case B* above gives

$S_2^2 = 84.0 \times 10^{-9} \, pA^2$

$S_1^2 = 1.22 \times 10^{-9} \, pA^2$

and

$F = 68.8$.

Thus in this case the two methods of calculating F do not agree, although both show that the results are not homogeneous.

Appendix 4

The weighted mean and standard error of grouped data

As discussed on page 7, there are occasions when repeated observations on a physical quantity are made in groups rather than in a single consecutive series and this appendix shows how these observations can be combined to determine the overall mean and its standard error. There are assumed to be n observations arranged in r groups. The jth group has n_j observations, the value of the ith observation in that group is y_{ij} and is given a weight w_{ij}.

The values of the observations within the groups will show a dispersion because of random fluctuations giving rise to differences in both the mean values and the standard errors of the means of the different groups. If systematic changes have occurred between the groups, then the variability between the mean values and standard errors of the groups may be different from that predicted from the variability of the individual observations. To check this the data can be examined for self consistency using the significance tests described in Appendix 3.

Self consistent data

If the data are self consistent then the mean value of the jth group is

$$\bar{y}_j = \frac{\sum_{i=1}^{n_j} w_{ij} y_{ij}}{\sum_{i=1}^{n_j} w_{ij}}, \qquad [A.4.1]$$

the overall mean is

$$\bar{y} = \frac{\sum_{j=1}^{r} \sum_{i=1}^{n_j} w_{ij} y_{ij}}{\sum_{j=1}^{r} \sum_{i=1}^{n_j} w_{ij}} \qquad [A.4.2]$$

and the variance of the overall mean is

$$S^2(\bar{y}) = \frac{\sum_{j=1}^{r} \sum_{i=1}^{n_j} w_{ij}(y_{ij} - \bar{y})^2}{(n-1) \sum_{j=1}^{r} \sum_{i=1}^{n_j} w_{ij}}. \qquad [A.4.3]$$

In Appendix 3, the quantities S_1^2 and S_2^2 were defined in equations A.3.3.1 and A.3.3.2. It can be shown that

$$S^2(\bar{y}) = \frac{n-r}{n-1} S_1^2 + \frac{r-1}{n-1} S_2^2,$$

and when $S_1 \approx S_2$, or when $n_j \gtrsim 10$, then

$$S^2(\bar{y}) \approx S_1^2 = \frac{\displaystyle\sum_{j=1}^{r} \sum_{i=1}^{n_j} w_{ij}(y_{ij}-\bar{y}_j)^2}{(n-r) \displaystyle\sum_{j=1}^{r} \sum_{i=1}^{n_j} w_{ij}} \quad . \qquad [\text{A.4.4}]$$

There remains the problem of choosing the appropriate weights, w_{ij}. Two cases were discussed in Section A.3.3. In both these cases the observations within any one group are given equal weight, and therefore for the jth group:

$$\bar{y}_j = \frac{1}{n_j} \sum_{i=1}^{n_j} y_{ij} \qquad [\text{A.4.5}]$$

$$S^2(y_j) = \frac{1}{n_j-1} \sum_{i=1}^{n_j} (y_{ij}-\bar{y}_j)^2 \qquad [\text{A.4.6}]$$

and

$$S^2(\bar{y}_j) = \frac{1}{n_j} S^2(y_j) \quad . \qquad [\text{A.4.7}]$$

Case A There is found to be no significant difference between the means or the variances of the groups. Here all the observations are then given the same weight.

From equation A.4.2

$$\bar{y} = \frac{1}{n} \sum_{j=1}^{r} \sum_{i=1}^{n_j} y_{ij} = \frac{1}{n} \sum_{j=1}^{r} n_j \bar{y}_j \quad . \qquad [\text{A.4.8}]$$

From equation A.4.3

$$S^2(\bar{y}) = \frac{1}{n(n-1)} \sum_{j=1}^{r} \sum_{i=1}^{n_j} (y_{ij}-\bar{y})^2 \qquad [\text{A.4.9}]$$

with $n-1$ degrees of freedom,

or from equation A.4.4

$$S^2(\bar{y}) \approx \frac{1}{n(n-r)} \sum_{j=1}^{r} \sum_{i=1}^{n_j} (y_{ij}-\bar{y}_j)^2 \qquad [\text{A.4.10}]$$

For the very common situation in which just two sets of data have to be combined the above formulae become

$$\bar{y} = \frac{n_1 \bar{y}_1 + n_2 \bar{y}_2}{n_1 + n_2}$$

[A.4.8a]

$$S^2(\bar{y}) = \frac{(n_1 - 1) S^2(y_1) + (n_2 - 1) S^2(y_2) + n_1 n_2 (\bar{y}_1 - \bar{y}_2)^2/(n_1 + n_2)}{(n_1 + n_2)(n_1 + n_2 - 1)}$$

[A.4.9a]

$$S^2(\bar{y}) \approx \frac{(n_1 - 1) S^2(y_1) + (n_2 - 1) S^2(y_2)}{(n_1 + n_2)(n_1 + n_2 - 2)} .$$

[A.4.10a]

Case B There is found to be no significant difference between the mean values of the groups but the standard deviations of the groups differ significantly from each other. Then all observations in a group are given the same weight, and this weight is usually derived from the estimate of the variance of that group. This method should be used only when an F test shows clearly that the standard deviations of the groups differ significantly and there are reasonable grounds from physical reasoning to explain these differences. For example, it would be an appropriate method to use to combine the results from a number of experiments carried out in different ways at different times.

In this case $w_{ij} = w_j$ is normally taken as $1/S^2(y_j)$.

From equation A.4.2

$$\bar{y} = \frac{\sum_{j=1}^{r} w_j \sum_{i=1}^{n_j} y_{ij}}{\sum_{j=1}^{r} n_j w_j} = \frac{\sum_{j=1}^{r} \bar{y}_j/S^2(\bar{y}_j)}{\sum_{j=1}^{r} 1/S^2(\bar{y}_j)} .$$

[A.4.11]

From equation A.4.3

$$S^2(\bar{y}) = \frac{\sum_{j=1}^{r} \sum_{i=1}^{n_j} (y_{ij} - \bar{y})^2/S^2(y_j)}{(n-1) \sum_{j=1}^{r} n_j/S^2(y_j)}$$

[A.4.12]

with $n-1$ degrees of freedom,

or from equation A.4.4

$$S^2(\bar{y}) \approx \frac{1}{\sum_{j=1}^{r} 1/S^2(\bar{y}_j)} .$$

[A.4.13]

45

Again for just two sets of data which have to be combined the above formulae become:

$$\bar{y} = \frac{\bar{y}_1 S^2(\bar{y}_2) + \bar{y}_2 S^2(\bar{y}_1)}{S^2(\bar{y}_2) + S^2(\bar{y}_1)} \qquad \text{[A.4.11a]}$$

$$\frac{1}{S^2(\bar{y})} \approx \frac{1}{S^2(\bar{y}_1)} + \frac{1}{S^2(\bar{y}_2)} \qquad . \qquad \text{[A.4.13a]}$$

Data that are not self consistent

If an F test shows that the variation between the means of the groups of measurements is not consistent with the variation within the groups then this implies that the experimental conditions changed between the groups. Under these circumstances, neither of the methods of choosing weights described above would be appropriate, for in *Case A* unjustifiable weight would be given to a group with a large number of observations, while in *Case B* unjustifiable weight would be given to a group which has a high precision. Ideally, the reasons for the inconsistencies should be investigated and their causes eliminated. However, if this is not possible or is unsuccessful, then, provided that the distribution of mean values is consistent with the Normal law, the best measure of the dispersion of the results is derived from the dispersion of the mean values of the groups, and the mean values of the groups are treated effectively as if they were single observations.

Then

$$\bar{y} = \frac{1}{r} \sum_{j=1}^{r} \bar{y}_j, \qquad \text{[A.4.14]}$$

and

$$S^2(\bar{y}) = \frac{1}{r(r-1)} \sum_{j=1}^{r} (\bar{y}_j - \bar{y})^2 \qquad \text{[A.4.15]}$$

with $r-1$ degrees of freedom and where $\bar{y}_j$ is given by equation A.4.5.

Another situation arises when the frequency distribution of the mean values is not Normal, or when there are insufficient mean values to prove Normality. In such cases the data should be examined for correlations and, if possible, corrections applied. If no correlation can be found the data should be treated with reserve.

Tables

Table 1

Test	Hypothesis
χ^2	The numbers (o) of observations falling into k classes do not differ significantly from expected numbers (e) [total number expected made to agree with total number observed and the l parameters needed to define the distribution are estimated from the observations]
t	The means $\bar{y}_1$ and $\bar{y}_2$ of n_1 and n_2 observations do not differ significantly (standard deviations estimated from samples)
F	One variance S_1^2 estimated from n_1 observations is not significantly greater than another S_2^2 estimated from n_2 observations

Adapted, with permission, from KAYE, G. W. and LABY, T. H. *Tables of Physical and Chemical Constants*, 13th edition, Longmans, Green and Co. Ltd, 1966.

Function	Cell of Table 2	
	N_1	N_2
$$\frac{\chi^2}{(k-l-1)} = \sum_{i=1}^{k} \{(o_i - e_i)^2/e_i\}/(k-l-1)$$	$k-l-1$	∞
$$_2 = \frac{n_1 n_2}{n_1 + n_2} \left(\frac{\bar{y}_1 - \bar{y}_2}{S}\right)^2$$ where $$S^2 = \frac{1}{n_1 + n_2 - 2}\left[\sum_{i=1}^{n_1}(y_i - \bar{y}_1)^2 + \sum_{j=1}^{n_2}(y_j - \bar{y}_2)^2\right]$$ $$= \frac{1}{n_1 + n_2 - 2}[n_1(n_1 - 1)S^2(\bar{y}_1) + n_2(n_2 - 1)S^2(\bar{y}_2)]$$	1	$n_1 + n_2 - 2$
$$\mathcal{F} = S_1^2/S_2^2$$ where $$_1^2 = \sum_{i=1}^{n_1}(y_i - \bar{y}_1)^2/n_1 - 1, \text{ etc.}$$	$n_1 - 1$	$n_2 - 1$

Table 2

The three rows for each value of N_2 correspond to values of $P = 0.95$, 0.99 and 0.999 respectively; the values for $P = 0.99$ are printed in bold type

N_2 \ N_1	1	2	3	4	5	6	8	12	24	∞
1	161.4	199.5	215.7	224.6	230.2	234.0	238.9	243.9	249.0	254.3
	4052	**4999**	**5403**	**5625**	**5764**	**5859**	**5981**	**6106**	**6234**	**6366**
	Values for $P=0.999$ too large for entry									
2	18.5	19.0	19.2	19.2	19.3	19.3	19.4	19.4	19.4	19.5
	98.5	**99.0**	**99.2**	**99.2**	**99.3**	**99.3**	**99.4**	**99.4**	**99.5**	**99.5**
	998.5	999.0	999.2	999.2	999.3	999.3	999.4	999.4	999.5	999.5
3	10.1	9.6	9.3	9.1	9.0	8.9	8.8	8.7	8.6	8.5
	34.1	**30.8**	**29.5**	**28.7**	**28.2**	**27.9**	**27.5**	**27.0**	**26.6**	**26.1**
	167.0	148.5	141.1	137.1	134.6	132.8	130.6	128.3	125.9	123.5
4	7.7	6.9	6.6	6.4	6.3	6.2	6.0	5.9	5.8	5.6
	21.2	**18.0**	**16.7**	**16.0**	**15.5**	**15.2**	**14.8**	**14.4**	**13.9**	**13.5**
	74.1	61.2	56.2	53.4	51.7	50.5	49.0	47.4	45.8	44.0
5	6.6	5.8	5.4	5.2	5.0	5.0	4.8	4.7	4.5	4.4
	16.3	**13.3**	**12.1**	**11.4**	**11.0**	**10.7**	**10.3**	**9.9**	**9.5**	**9.0**
	47.2	37.1	33.2	31.1	29.8	28.8	27.6	26.4	25.1	23.8
6	6.0	5.1	4.8	4.5	4.4	4.3	4.1	4.0	3.8	3.7
	13.7	**10.9**	**9.8**	**9.2**	**8.8**	**8.5**	**8.1**	**7.7**	**7.3**	**6.9**
	35.5	27.0	23.7	21.9	20.8	20.0	19.0	18.0	16.9	15.8
7	5.6	4.7	4.3	4.1	4.0	3.9	3.7	3.6	3.4	3.2
	12.2	**9.6**	**8.4**	**7.8**	**7.5**	**7.2**	**6.8**	**6.5**	**6.1**	**5.6**
	29.2	21.7	18.8	17.2	16.2	15.5	14.6	13.7	12.7	11.7
8	5.3	4.5	4.1	3.8	3.7	3.6	3.4	3.3	3.1	2.9
	11.3	**8.6**	**7.6**	**7.0**	**6.6**	**6.4**	**6.0**	**5.7**	**5.3**	**4.9**
	25.4	18.5	15.8	14.4	13.5	12.9	12.0	11.2	10.3	9.3
9	5.1	4.3	3.9	3.6	3.5	3.4	3.2	3.1	2.9	2.7
	10.6	**8.0**	**7.0**	**6.4**	**6.1**	**5.8**	**5.5**	**5.1**	**4.7**	**4.3**
	22.9	16.4	13.9	12.6	11.7	11.1	10.4	9.6	8.7	7.8
10	5.0	4.1	3.7	3.5	3.3	3.2	3.1	2.9	2.7	2.5
	10.0	**7.6**	**6.6**	**6.0**	**5.6**	**5.4**	**5.1**	**4.7**	**4.3**	**3.9**
	21.0	14.9	12.6	11.3	10.5	9.9	9.2	8.4	7.6	6.8
11	4.8	4.0	3.6	3.4	3.2	3.1	2.9	2.8	2.6	2.4
	9.6	**7.2**	**6.2**	**5.7**	**5.3**	**5.1**	**4.7**	**4.4**	**4.0**	**3.6**
	19.7	13.8	11.6	10.4	9.6	9.0	8.4	7.6	6.8	6.0
12	4.8	3.9	3.5	3.3	3.1	3.0	2.8	2.7	2.5	2.3
	9.3	**6.9**	**6.0**	**5.4**	**5.1**	**4.8**	**4.5**	**4.2**	**3.8**	**3.4**
	18.6	13.0	10.8	9.6	8.9	8.4	7.7	7.0	6.2	5.4
13	4.7	3.8	3.4	3.2	3.0	2.9	2.8	2.6	2.4	2.2
	9.1	**6.7**	**5.7**	**5.2**	**4.9**	**4.6**	**4.3**	**4.0**	**3.6**	**3.2**
	17.8	12.3	10.2	9.1	8.4	7.9	7.2	6.5	5.8	5.0
14	4.6	3.7	3.3	3.1	3.0	2.8	2.7	2.5	2.4	2.1
	8.9	**6.5**	**5.6**	**5.0**	**4.7**	**4.5**	**4.1**	**3.8**	**3.4**	**3.0**
	17.1	11.8	9.7	8.6	7.9	7.4	6.8	6.1	5.4	4.6

N_2 \ N_1	1	2	3	4	5	6	8	12	24	∞
15	4.5	3.7	3.3	3.1	2.9	2.8	2.6	2.5	2.3	2.1
	8.7	**6.4**	**5.4**	**4.9**	**4.6**	**4.3**	**4.0**	**3.7**	**3.3**	**2.9**
	16.6	11.3	9.3	8.2	7.6	7.1	6.5	5.8	5.1	4.3
16	4.5	3.6	3.2	3.0	2.9	2.7	2.6	2.4	2.2	2.0
	8.5	**6.2**	**5.3**	**4.8**	**4.4**	**4.2**	**3.9**	**3.6**	**3.2**	**2.8**
	16.1	11.0	9.0	7.9	7.3	6.8	6.2	5.6	4.8	4.1
17	4.5	3.6	3.2	3.0	2.8	2.7	2.5	2.4	2.2	2.0
	8.4	**6.1**	**5.2**	**4.7**	**4.3**	**4.1**	**3.8**	**3.4**	**3.1**	**2.6**
	15.7	10.7	8.7	7.7	7.0	6.6	6.0	5.3	4.6	3.8
18	4.4	3.6	3.2	2.9	2.8	2.7	2.5	2.3	2.1	1.9
	8.3	**6.0**	**5.1**	**4.6**	**4.2**	**4.0**	**3.7**	**3.4**	**3.0**	**2.6**
	15.4	10.4	8.5	7.5	6.8	6.4	5.8	5.1	4.4	3.7
19	4.4	3.5	3.1	2.9	2.7	2.6	2.5	2.3	2.1	1.9
	8.2	**5.9**	**5.0**	**4.5**	**4.2**	**3.9**	**3.6**	**3.3**	**2.9**	**2.5**
	15.1	10.2	8.3	7.3	6.6	6.2	5.6	5.0	4.3	3.5
20	4.4	3.5	3.1	2.9	2.7	2.6	2.4	2.3	2.1	1.8
	8.1	**5.8**	**4.9**	**4.4**	**4.1**	**3.9**	**3.6**	**3.2**	**2.9**	**2.4**
	14.8	10.0	8.1	7.1	6.5	6.0	5.4	4.8	4.2	3.4
22	4.3	3.4	3.0	2.8	2.7	2.6	2.4	2.2	2.0	1.8
	7.9	**5.7**	**4.8**	**4.3**	**4.0**	**3.8**	**3.4**	**3.1**	**2.8**	**2.3**
	14.4	9.6	7.8	6.8	6.2	5.8	5.2	4.6	3.9	3.2
24	4.3	3.4	3.0	2.8	2.6	2.5	2.4	2.2	2.0	1.7
	7.8	**5.6**	**4.7**	**4.2**	**3.9**	**3.7**	**3.4**	**3.0**	**2.7**	**2.2**
	14.0	9.3	7.6	6.6	6.0	5.6	5.0	4.4	3.7	3.0
26	4.2	3.4	3.0	2.7	2.6	2.5	2.3	2.2	1.9	1.7
	7.7	**5.5**	**4.6**	**4.1**	**3.8**	**3.6**	**3.3**	**3.0**	**2.6**	**2.1**
	13.7	9.1	7.4	6.4	5.8	5.4	4.8	4.2	3.6	2.8
28	4.2	3.3	3.0	2.7	2.6	2.4	2.3	2.1	1.9	1.6
	7.6	**5.4**	**4.6**	**4.1**	**3.8**	**3.5**	**3.2**	**2.9**	**2.5**	**2.1**
	13.5	8.9	7.2	6.2	5.7	5.2	4.7	4.1	3.5	2.7
30	4.2	3.3	2.9	2.7	2.5	2.4	2.3	2.1	1.9	1.6
	7.6	**5.4**	**4.5**	**4.0**	**3.7**	**3.5**	**3.2**	**2.8**	**2.5**	**2.0**
	13.3	8.8	7.0	6.1	5.5	5.1	4.6	4.0	3.4	2.6
40	4.1	3.2	2.8	2.6	2.4	2.3	2.2	2.0	1.8	1.5
	7.3	**5.2**	**4.3**	**3.8**	**3.5**	**3.3**	**3.0**	**2.7**	**2.3**	**1.8**
	12.6	8.2	6.6	5.7	5.1	4.7	4.2	3.6	3.0	2.2
60	4.0	3.2	2.8	2.5	2.4	2.2	2.1	1.9	1.7	1.4
	7.1	**5.0**	**4.1**	**3.6**	**3.3**	**3.1**	**2.8**	**2.5**	**2.1**	**1.6**
	12.0	7.8	6.2	5.3	4.8	4.4	3.9	3.3	2.7	1.9
120	3.9	3.1	2.7	2.4	2.3	2.2	2.0	1.8	1.6	1.2
	6.8	**4.8**	**4.0**	**3.5**	**3.2**	**3.0**	**2.7**	**2.3**	**2.0**	**1.4**
	11.4	7.3	5.8	5.0	4.4	4.0	3.6	3.0	2.4	1.5
∞	3.8	3.0	2.6	2.4	2.2	2.1	1.9	1.8	1.5	1.0
	6.6	**4.6**	**3.8**	**3.3**	**3.0**	**2.8**	**2.5**	**2.2**	**1.8**	**1.0**
	10.8	6.9	5.4	4.6	4.1	3.7	3.3	2.7	2.1	1.0

Adapted from Table V of Fisher and Yates; *Statistical Tables for Biological, Agricultural and Medical Research* (6th edition 1963) published by Oliver and Boyd, Edinburgh, by permission of the authors and publishers.

Table 3
Values of t for various values of the confidence level P

Degrees of freedom (v)	$P = 68.3\%$ (1σ)	$P = 95\%$	$P = 99\%$	$P = 99.73\%$ (3σ)
(1)	(1.8)	(12.7)	(64)	(235)
2	1.32	4.30	9.9	19.2
3	1.20	3.18	5.8	9.2
4	1.15	2.78	4.6	6.6
5	1.11	2.57	4.0	5.5
6	1.09	2.45	3.7	4.9
7	1.08	2.37	3.5	4.5
8	1.07	2.31	3.4	4.3
9	1.06	2.26	3.2	4.1
10	1.05	2.23	3.2	4.0
15	1.03	2.13	3.0	3.6
20	1.03	2.09	2.8	3.4
30	1.02	2.04	2.8	3.3
50	1.01	2.01	2.7	3.2
100	1.00	1.98	2.6	3.1
200	1.00	1.97	2.6	3.0
∞	1.00	1.96	2.58	3.0

Printed in England for Her Majesty's Stationery Office
by William Clowes & Sons Limited, London, Colchester and Beccles
Dd 504612 K14 5/73